FABER NEW POE

CW00429495

IN THE SAME SERIES

1 — FIONA BENSON

2 — TOBY MARTINEZ DE LAS RIVAS

3 — HEATHER PHILLIPSON

4 — JACK UNDERWOOD

5 — JOE DUNTHORNE

6 — ANNIE KATCHINSKA

7 — SAM RIVIERE

8 — TOM WARNER

9 — RACHAEL ALLEN

10 — WILL BURNS

11 — ZAFFAR KUNIAL

12 — DECLAN RYAN

Rachael Allen

FABER & FABER

First published in 2014
by Faber & Faber Ltd
Bloomsbury House
74–77 Great Russell Street
London WC1B 3DA

Typeset by Hamish Ironside
Printed in England by Abbeystar

ACKNOWLEDGEMENTS

Thank you to the editors of *The White Review*, *Poetry London*,
Five Dials, *Stop Sharpening Your Knives*, *Dear World & Everyone
In It* and *The Salt Book of Younger Poets*, who first published some
of these poems. Thanks also to Sam Buchan-Watts, Jack Underwood,
Sophie Collins, Sam Riviere, Lukus Roberts, Andrew Parkes, Harriet
Moore, Harry Burke, Rye Holmboe, Oli Hazzard, Parisa Ebrahimi,
Hannah Barry and my friends and family for their help with my poems.

A CIP record for this book
is available from the British Library

ISBN 978-0-571-32120-9

2 4 6 8 10 9 7 5 3 1

Contents

Goonhilly 1

Random 2

Kingdomland 3

Cute/Male 4

Polruan 5

Transportation 6

The Slim Man 7

Animu & Mango 8

Regional Tendencies 9

Rapidshares 10

Sunday 11

Sexy Beautiful Women 12

Early Harbour 13

Social 14

I 15

Science & Math 16

Old Fears Are Still Valid 17

Goonhilly

It is 1978 and there's the woman before my mother
behind that flimsy bank glass. She is called Miss Heather
and is a delicately translucent clerk, rinsed out but luminous
with hope. One work evening, you are to take her
to that forest of satellites, where the future ideas of us are
    mocking you
from behind whacked-out nuclear trees.

As the evening sun greets those farcical discs
hold the small of her back and draw her gently to you
(smelling lily of the valley and copper).
She asks about radar and you will conclude it is dangerous
and feeling the weight of a memory about to happen
you tell her so, *isn't anything we can't see?*

Random
/b/

Boxxy you are the home of the anonymous. I liked to read on you all my false news – it went across your head like The Financial District and how you glowed with it. I got Tippex and painted you as an angel on my childhood rucksack and wore you proudly to school – you've got the kind of fame of girls who killed other girls in childhood. I wonder if you've ever seen lampposts in LA? Do they have crabs where you are? Sometimes everyone thinks you're dead. I saw a rainbow today but it had nothing on you. Your eyes held entire months of teenage summers when my skin smelt of a scented diary from the garden centre or an Impulse set from Safeways – anyway I think where we lost you was somewhere in the Californian sun squint and glare.

Kingdomland

At the rise of the moon
bells fade out
and impassable paths
appear.
– FEDERICO GARCÍA LORCA, 'The Moon Appears'

The dark village sits on the crooked hill.
There is a plot of impassable paths towards it,
impassable paths overcome with bees, the stigma that bees bring.
There is a bottleneck at the base of the hive.
There is an impassable knowledge that your eyebrows bring.
   Beside the poor library
and the wicker-man, there's a man who sells peacock feathers on
   the roundabout,
they scream all night from where they are plucked.
The village is slanted, full of tragedies with slate.

I am walking towards a level crossing, while someone I love is
   jogging into the darkness.
Come away from there, I am yelling,
while the black dog rolls in the twilit yard.
Small white socks bob into the dark like teeth in the mouth of a
   laughing man
who walks backwards into night, throwing drinks into the air
like a superstitious wife throws salt; we all have our share of
   certainties.
The glass and salt my petulant daughter,
the glass and salt my crooked pathway; impassable glass and salt.

Cute/Male
/cm/

When we play *The Simpsons* game where I find an episode of
The Simpsons that is like real life, I think about the presence of
that squeeze of our shared childhood spent however many
miles apart and I imagine us both rooted to a Sunday television
with porcelain swans, a baby gumming on a cork coaster with
mottled animals on it – aching bored afternoons spent
grappling with our siblings – this was when our lives were
never ending, gazing out of windows into suburbs where the
pink dusk settles like a trapping net. Maybe once our eyes met
through a satellite or something I think maybe that's too
romantic – how about you give me a picture of a verge of grass
and a stream, I'll show you there we are those tiny dots

Polruan

To think that pool of guppies needle-threading
through the weed crags of the tidal pool, as pushing now
to blank, deep ocean, is incompatible with what I see
from my place on the cliff's terse angle.

The sea's a lurching drunk, savaging itself so we are blind
to what's beneath. On one surf's curve, I glimpse a band
of iridescence layering under foam, as though they work to
mirror sky, and then a Möbius strip of light: a glint, continuous.

Transportation
/n/

Mother says 'Why ask and re-ask questions!' but I'm so often unsure of the question asked especially when it's the models of cars, and you must understand I had lessons for a very long time and I still don't know the difference between one shift and another. Before traffic lights and crowd control people used to march grinning right in front of the bonnet – straight into traffic! Like how I once saw so many translucent frogs being swept downstream glassy-eyed and knowing towards the open mouth of a drain, their eyes were so resigned that I even gave some a little push, the driving instructor gave me similar looks of resignation, lorries never seem so big in stasis, I'm sorry what was the question?

The Slim Man

A landscape unpainted:
a cold stream of lean black weeds
leading towards a stile
and a field tilting up.
Trees turn to veins against marbly sky
in the half hour before night.

During a certain moon
children are said to have seen
a slim man walking over the field
in a low mist, towards the stile,
leading a girl
in pale blue pinstripes
into the glowing pinstripe forest beyond.

Sometimes he will stop and lean down,
and scrape the earth,
then earth and touch are knotted
for they are both cold.
No one is scared of him,
more of the thick dark brook, drowned roots
and full night, the pitiful rabbits'
eyes yellow on the hillside.

Animu & Mango

/a/

The main bit's where Naru and Keitaro kiss and in character Keitaro was Declan who lived in Pensilva and had a cast and wore school uniform even after school (poor) and I was Naru. In one scene I made Declan promise we'd go away to college together but I don't think he understood, we were far beyond the slap-pink and heavy breathing of a slow Chinese burn but would carry on doing them in silence or burn shag bands on hay bales that were shrink-wrapped in the nearly dark and as he burnt grass I dreamt heavily and cleanly about our future together it was in truth a sluggish start anyway he's in the navy now and probably knows how to make a promise.

Regional Tendencies

The fathers are half shame
half salesmen
and go from door to door
discounting their shame
with counted flirtation
with married women

who bat at them
with telling hands
and look down
while somehow also looking
up. The village is a cesspit
for this kind of thing.

A torso-sized portrait
of beautiful Alison
hangs in the house next door.
It's badly painted
acrylic and lopsided.
She's looking over her shoulder.

My father is more shame
than father.
He bounces us on the knee
he bounces other women on
perhaps Alison, perhaps not.
The light in the village

is lilac and patient.
I'm always expecting
something to happen.

Rapidshares

/rs/

Gina G was the pathway to enlightenment and adulthood
another of the pathways was my pink faux-snakeskin halter
neck top that came free with a magazine and I shimmied it on,
it was skinny and violently pink like someone embarrassed,
feeling older, I thought thirty, and drinking too much Sprite
when someone shouted from across the beery carpets 'that
top looks like something you'd get free from a magazine' and
for some reason I was insulted and girls that strutted
and gathered like pigeons patted my back and we puffed out our
flat chests for the rest of the evening, skittering on our low
heels playing at adulthood and anger and all around me was
ooh ahh and *de de da da da* and a tacky smell of sweets that
could have been lipgloss or just as easily the encroaching ledge
of age.

Sunday

Supermarket Warehouse

This is the ornate layer: in the supermarket warehouse,
boxed children's gardens rocking on a forklift truck,
two rats rutting as a closed door would be punched over
and over again (we are locked out: the paddling pools
are torture saying *Florida! Florida! Florida!* forever).
The toys come alive to 'Für Elise' as they do in our
combined nightmares, daring each other, spinning on
stray dust leaked into crates, making waves of fur.

Camping in the Supermarket Garden

Outside, the motorway is humming with the night shift
but it is not luminescent or romantic like the glow-gore
of signs in America that say M O T E L. Instead, the
burnt stubble of wildness: low-lying spinney and shrub,
the gradual fallout from car crashes, over-age tent-shares
or over-age friendship. Unpacked beer for goose-pimpled
men loud with drink, their eyes wide and pale all night.

Home

We go back on Sundays to our Tamblin Avenues and
Hollyhock Gardens, blooming with the fire smell, taking
our shoes off, picking up our tiny babies, having baths.
While sitting, we flick through the catalogue. Watching,
a tight teal or sea-blue orient-themed wall frieze, a waist-
belt Millennium hangover, keeping it in. A cat squats and
quivers as it craps in the bushes. Now on the quiet estate
we are cooking, rest assured things will stay as they are.

Sexy Beautiful Women

/s/

When Nicola's mother remarried that brutish farmer she
started growing a leafy bedroom drawer of unmarked VHSs
and on a sun-trapped estate afternoon we sat transfixed with
shop sweets and gluey underarms as circus lesbians wrapped
themselves around snakes and medieval women ate raw hides
of meat and then later Erica Lopez's cam (*Squirting Tease Party
Erica*) accidentally came up and it was a glittering, stuttering
throwback to some damp afternoons of slow awakening
anyway there's moar if you want it pages and pages of Ericas
so many Ericas you may forget that they're sort of real
somewhere in the world in real life

Early Harbour

The horizon is a line-white flare;
boats lead in over the flat
as though on a conveyor belt.

Fish garble in the filaments of rope,
whacking metronomic
with their unblinking dial eyes

rapidly drying
to a firm gel. I imagine being cabled
in the base of the net,

slapping madly for what is inside me,
something not yet blinking or rhythmic
but locked in, laying low.

The firm, acrid hospital seat
is the burnt orange
of rough wire. I steer you too early,

unnecessary creature.
Fish heave, the sea heaves,
I mete out the likeness as tidal.

Social
/soc/

The reason is probably because she started to watch all these day programmes, first about Aileen Wuornos and then about murderers in general, but she really loved the show called *The Unthinkable – Children who Kill and What Motivates Them.* She'd tell me about the murders, the intricate planning and 'aren't they heartless' as though challenging me, and while ironing, so the steam would fatten and cloud her face

but the other reason is probably my father who was a library of frustrations but didn't drink, instead he ate arguments until his stomach bloated like a cupcake's foamy middle because he was *exhausted* with all of us, but once that calmed down they went back to normal, like maybe child-killers and mini-strokes are modern lobotomies, but I was scarred for life that's probably two of the reasons.

I

Something is flying over our VHS shop,
over the key cutters and blank stones.
Why is no one as terrified as me?
We aim our tennis balls into
the darkness. We do not
know what makes
the moon.

We take turns with the holy remote
in crepuscular front rooms.
Villages mushroom up
around our village,
what happens,
nothing.

*

There is no heart on the circular road
there is no heart in the car park
the roundabout beats like
a palpitating throat.

It is a linked and endless map, built as
a child's toy with its simplicity
of instruction. Stop, go this
way, don't go that.

Science & Math
/sci/

Dear Mr Mitchell and Mrs Snell

       sorry for drawing upside-
down triangles in the back of my exercise books and turning
them into the most angular nude women with tufty bottoms
and circle breasts I promise that I was doing my best to balance
something or other against the state of stress at the points
against something

           the thing is
my mother would step out of the bath each evening unashamed
and frosted with bubbles and even though her body was my
body I was yet to see these rings of flesh as mine she was so
heat-speckled

        so at the same time as clumsy
fresh boys were fizzing hair on the Bunsen burner I was
debating what of mine would fill the planet-sized bra on the
landing and when

Old Fears Are Still Valid

I hold you only when I think too clearly.
I was told I have a bright future ahead of me
but I think it's now, or I'm using it all up.
The school teacher disallowed my Etnies and since then
I've had a personal vendetta;
the receiving end of it is myself.
In my dreams you comment on my slouch.
You sick litter-box, stinky dog-bin,
half-arsed daffodil, hair-gel smell from the new leaves.
There's cotton discharge on the fumes,
the blood of my sister in the flume.
I don't have a Mercedes childhood
and poor Tom's a coke-head,
where's my text from the Office of the Dead?
I see an open bit of land from where
the estuary is torn apart; how can a landscape change
to reflect so suddenly the breaking of a person – it's bread.
The earth is drier than it was. One digger is staccato,
glances are exchanged like fish.
The birds are bloated with plastic.
Glances between my parents switch into the river
and remain there. A washing machine tumbles down the hillside –
it isn't representative.
This is where they dump the household waste.
There was no council to decide but
there's much to administrate.
There is still skin on the black asphalt.
Cotton panties hem your thigh,
loud and little like the shouting of a child.
Cotton ferns hem the fence.
What's that light on the horizon, the one we always head to?
Bus station, flatlands, LED cloud, TEXACO.